# Pure & Simple

A cookbook in four seasons.

LUND FOOD HOLDINGS, INC.

**Lund Food Holdings, Inc.**
President and CEO: Russell T. Lund III
Executive Chefs: Dave Barber, Todd Callander,
   Paul Supplee, Tim Tesch
Creative Director: Barb Birr
Recipe Editor: Bea James, Deidre Schipani
Copy Editor: Michelle Croteau
Nutritional Editor: Kari Shifflett
Recipe Testers: Culinary Specialists
Production: Amanda Engquist, Shelly Sunde
Design: Morgan Williams & Associates, Inc.
Food Photographer: Mette Nielsen
Food Stylist: Robin Krause
Prop Stylist: Michele Joy
Printing: Litho Inc.

# Pure & Simple

Conceived and produced by Lund Food Holdings, Inc.
4100 West 50th Street, Edina, Minnesota 55424

# Contents

**Living Wise**

Choices *for Your* Health

# A Few Words about Living Wise™

With every season comes change. Behind every extraordinary meal are great recipes. In every book, there is a message. The message of our cookbook is Living Wise.

In designing our store-wide health and wellness program, we combined two traditional and basic concepts — premium natural products with healthy living. Our result is an innovative program for our customers designed specifically to help support the relationship between health, nutrition and mind-body. We call the program Living Wise.

*Executive Chefs Tim Tesch, Dave Barber, Todd Callander and Paul Supplee.*

In creating our first Living Wise cookbook, we took extraordinary care to ensure that our recipes are of superior quality in both ingredients and taste. Our executive chefs combined their expertise to design tasteful menus that wonderfully represent each of the four seasons. For each recipe, they selected ingredients that were natural, organic whenever possible and of premium quality — meeting the Living Wise criteria. Our team of culinary specialists then tested each delicious creation in our test kitchen to guarantee user-friendly recipes.

We present to you a compilation of personal masterpieces.

# Spring Menu

Fresh Cilantro Jicama Salad

Thai Curry Chicken Breast
with Mango Sauce

Longevity Noodles

Olive Focaccia

Grilled Rum Pineapple
with Crème Fraîche

*Wine Recommendation*

Husch Gewurztraminer

Murphy-Goode Zinfandel

# Thai Curry Chicken Breast with Mango Sauce

*Yield:*
*Serves 4*

## Ingredients:

| 4 | | Boneless, Skinless Chicken Breasts |
|---|---|---|

**Marinade:**

| 1½ | tablespoons | Tamari Sauce |
|---|---|---|
| 1½ | tablespoons | Sugar |
| 1 | tablespoon | Fresh Ginger, minced |
| 1 | tablespoon | Fresh Garlic, minced |
| 2 | teaspoons | Thai Red Curry Paste |
| 1 | tablespoon | Fresh Lemongrass, minced |
| ¼ | cup | Orange Juice |
| 1 | tablespoon | Curry Powder |
| 1 | tablespoon | Sesame Oil |

**Sauce:**

| 1 | cup | Coconut Milk |
|---|---|---|
| 1 | tablespoon | Arrowroot |
| 2 | | Fresh, Ripe Mangoes, cut in ½ inch pieces |

## Preparation:

1. Combine marinade ingredients and add chicken. Let rest for at least 1 hour.

2. Remove chicken from marinade and place on a grill or sauté in skillet. Place marinade in a small saucepan over medium-high heat and bring to a boil. Combine coconut milk and arrowroot and slowly add to sauce. Bring back to a boil and reduce heat; simmer for 15 minutes.

3. When chicken is fully cooked, add mango to sauce. Place chicken on bed of rice or Asian-style noodles; spoon sauce over top and serve.

PER SERVING: Calories 300; Fat Calories 110; Total Fat 13g; Saturated Fat 8g; Cholesterol 65mg; Sodium 420mg; Total Carbohydrates 18g; Fiber 2g; Sugars 11g; Protein 29g

# Longevity Noodles

## Ingredients:

| | | |
|---|---|---|
| 1 | pound | Asian Egg Noodles or Vermicelli Pasta, cooked |
| ½ | pound | Snow Peapods, tips removed and cleaned |
| 1 | 3.5 oz pkg | Fresh Shiitake Mushrooms, cut in half, stems removed |
| 1 | 8 oz pkg | Bean Sprouts |
| 6 | | Green Onions, cut on the bias (at an angle) |
| 1 | small | Red Bell Pepper, sliced in thin strips |

Dressing:

| | | |
|---|---|---|
| 3 | tablespoons | Rice Vinegar |
| 3 | teaspoons | Chili Puree with Garlic |
| 2 | tablespoons | Tamari Sauce |
| 2 | tablespoons | Sugar |
| ¼ | teaspoon | Dried, Crushed Red Pepper |
| 1 | tablespoon | Toasted Sesame Seeds |
| 2 | tablespoons | Sesame Oil |
| 1 | tablespoon | Olive Oil |

## Chef's Tip:

*Because of their woody texture, be sure to remove the stems when preparing Shiitake mushrooms.*

*Yield: Serves 4-6*

## Preparation:

1. Prepare pasta and vegetables as specified.

2. Combine all ingredients. May be served as a salad or as a side dish. If served hot, heat wok or large sauté pan or fry pan, and add 2 tablespoons sesame oil. Add vegetables and stir until just tender. Add noodles and stir until heated through; add sauce and stir until well coated. Serve.

PER SERVING: Calories 120; Fat Calories 50; Total Fat 5g; Saturated Fat 1g; Cholesterol 10mg; Sodium 180mg; Total Carbohydrates 15g; Fiber 2g; Sugars 4g; Protein 3g

# Fresh Cilantro Jicama Salad

*Yield:*
*Serves 4-6*

## Ingredients:

| | | |
|---|---|---|
| 1 | large | Jicama, peeled and sliced in thin julienne strips (1$\frac{1}{2}$ pounds) |
| 1 | small | Yellow Bell Pepper, sliced in thin julienne strips |
| 1 | small | Red Bell Pepper, sliced in thin julienne strips |
| 1 | small | Red Onion, sliced in thin wedges |
| $\frac{1}{4}$ | cup | Cilantro, stem removed and chopped |
| $\frac{1}{4}$ | cup | White Wine Vinegar |
| $\frac{1}{3}$ | cup | Sugar |
| 1 | teaspoon | Pepper, coarsely ground |

## Preparation:

1. Prepare vegetables as specified and combine.

2. In separate bowl, combine vinegar, sugar and pepper. Stir to dissolve sugar. Pour over vegetables and serve.

PER SERVING: Calories 140; Fat Calories 0; Total Fat 0g; Sodium 15mg; Total Carbohydrates 33g; Fiber 4g; Sugars 18g; Protein 3g

# Olive Focaccia

Our Olive Focaccia is an Italian bread, rich with kalamata olives and Gruyère cheese.

# Grilled Rum Pineapple
## with Crème Fraîche

## Ingredients:

*Yield: Serves 4*

| | |
|---|---|
| 1 | Cored Pineapple |
| ¹/₂ cup | Dark Rum |
| 1 cup | Crème Fraîche |
| ¹/₄ cup | Honey |
| ¹/₄ cup | Macadamia Nuts, chopped, toasted |

## Preparation:

1. Cut pineapple into 12 wedges. Lay out in a shallow dish and pour on rum. Cover and marinate for at least 1 hour.

2. Whip crème fraîche and honey until stiff and holds shape.

3. Place wedges on grill and cook for about 6 minutes, turning once halfway through.

4. Serve pineapple warm with crème fraîche topping, garnished with macadamia nuts.

PER SERVING: Calories 240; Fat Calories 130; Total Fat 14g; Saturated Fat 6g; Cholesterol 30mg; Sodium 10mg; Total Carbohydrates 21g; Fiber 2g; Sugars 20g; Protein < 1g

## Chef's Tip:
*Whole fresh cored pineapples are available in the produce department.*

# Fresh Organic CHICKEN

When a product is organic, it generally means the item is raised and processed using methods that are friendly to our environment. Fresh Organic Chicken is a premium quality organic product selected on the basis of taste, purity and the manufacturer's integrity to support environmentally friendly production practices. Fresh organic chickens are all natural — raised on a free range, away from pesticides, antibiotics, artificial ingredients and growth stimulants. It's a natural product we consider Living Wise.

# Summer Menu

Summer Melon and Sweet Onion Salad

Grilled Sirloin
in Aged Balsamic Vinegar

Szechuan Long Beans

Roasted Garlic Bread

Summer Berry Rush

*Wine Recommendation*

Fess Parker Syrah

Markham Sauvignon Blanc

# Grilled Sirloin
# in Aged Balsamic Vinegar

*Yield:*
*Serves 4*

## Ingredients:

| | | |
|---|---|---|
| ¹/₂ | cup | Olive Oil |
| ¹/₂ | cup | Balsamic Vinegar |
| 1 | tablespoon | Fresh Thyme, de-stem, chopped coarse |
| 1 | tablespoon | Fresh Rosemary, stems removed, chopped coarse |
| 2 | teaspoons | Fresh Coarse Ground Black Pepper |
| 2-2¹/₂ | pounds | Thick Cut Sirloin |

## Preparation:

1. In food processor, add balsamic vinegar. Slowly add olive oil until emulsified. Add thyme, rosemary and pepper. Pulse to mix.

2. Place sirloin in large freezer bag. Pour marinade over. Remove as much air as possible; seal; and refrigerate for 12-24 hours. Bring to room temperature before grilling.

3. Light grill. When coals have white ash, place grate 4-5 inches from coals.

4. Grill steak 4 minutes. Turn ¹/₄ to make nice diamond pattern. Turn after about 8 minutes.

5. Grill second side approximately 8 minutes until internal temperature is 125 degrees for medium rare.

For sauce, place 1 cup balsamic vinegar in sauce pan (not aluminum). Bring to boil; lower heat to simmer; and reduce to 2 ounces. Pour over slices after carving.

PER SERVING: Calories 430; Fat Calories 260; Total Fat 29g; Saturated Fat 6g; Cholesterol 110mg; Sodium 105mg; Total Carbohydrates 4g; Sugars 3g; Protein 39g

## Chef's Tip:
*This recipe will work with your favorite cut of beef.*

# Szechuan Long Beans

## Ingredients:

| | | |
|---|---|---|
| 1 | 12 oz pkg | Green Beans, ends removed and cleaned |
| 1 | 3.5 oz pkg | Shiitake Mushrooms, stems removed |
| 2 | tablespoons | Sesame Seeds |
| 2 | tablespoons | Sesame Oil |
| 1 | tablespoon | Tamari Sauce |
| 1 | teaspoon | Sugar |
| 2 | teaspoons | Arrowroot |
| 1 | teaspoon | Chili Puree with Garlic |
| 1/2 | teaspoon | Dried, Crushed Red Pepper |
| 2 | tablespoons | Rice Vinegar |

*Yield:
Serves 4*

## Preparation:

1. Prepare mushrooms and measure out ingredients. Combine tamari sauce, sugar, arrowroot, chili puree, red pepper and rice vinegar; whisk together. Set aside.

2. Preheat electric or stovetop wok to high; add sesame oil. Using heat resistant spoon, coat wok with oil; add green beans. Stir frequently for about 2 minutes. Add mushrooms and sesame seeds. Stir until mushrooms begin to soften; add sauce and cook for an additional 2-3 minutes. Serve.

PER SERVING: Calories 110; Fat Calories 60; Total Fat 7g; Saturated Fat 1g; Sodium 1560mg; Total Carbohydrates 12g; Fiber 4g; Sugars 2g; Protein 4g

## Chef's Tip:
*Because mushrooms are porous, avoid soaking them in water. Instead, wash with a mushroom brush or terry cloth towel.*

# Horseradish

## Ingredients:

| | | |
|---|---|---|
| 1 | large | Horseradish Root, Fresh |
| 2 | tablespoons | White Vinegar |
| 2 | teaspoons | White Sugar (or honey) |
| 2 | tablespoons | Balsamic Vinegar |

## Preparation:

1. Peel root with potato peeler, then grate. Food processor is the fastest, but hand grater works well. Measure 1 cup grated horseradish root.

2. Place in bowl. Mix in sugar; let stand 5 minutes. Thoroughly mix in vinegar. Let stand for about 10 minutes before serving.

3. Sauté horseradish in balsamic vinegar.

4. Serve with steak.

# Summer Melon and Sweet Onion Salad

*Yield:*
*Serves 4*

## Ingredients:

| | | |
|---|---|---|
| 2 | cups | Seedless Watermelon, cut in 1 inch pieces |
| 2 | | Pepinos, peeled, seeded, cut in ¹/₂ inch pieces |
| 1 | small | Red Onion, thin slices |
| 6 | | Fresh Basil Leaves, cut into thin strips |
| 2 | tablespoons | Raspberry Vinegar |
| 4 | oz pkg | Baby Greens Kosher Salt and Pepper, to taste |

## Chef's Tip:

*Tastes great with poppy seed dressing.*

## Preparation:

1. Prepare items as stated. Gently toss together with vinegar and salt and pepper.

2. Line plate with about 2 cups of greens. Place 1 cup of melon mixture in center of greens. Garnish with a few small basil leaves.

PER SERVING: Calories 70; Total Fat 0g; Sodium 10mg; Total Carbohydrates 19g; Fiber 2g; Sugars 16g; Protein 2g

# Roasted Garlic

Our Roasted Garlic Bread combines classic sourdough with fresh garlic roasted in extra virgin olive oil.

# Summer Berry Rush

## Ingredients:

*Yield:*
*Serves 4*

| | | |
|---|---|---|
| 1 | pint | Yogurt |
| | | Zest of 1 Lime |
| 1/2 | cup | Organic Raisins |
| 1/2 | pint | Raspberries |
| 4 | | Strawberries, sliced |
| 3/4 | cup | Blueberries |
| 1/2 | cup | Granola |
| 4 | tablespoons | Honey |

## Preparation:

1. Mix yogurt, lime zest and organic raisins.

2. Divide yogurt into 4 dishes. Combine fruit. Top each dish with 1/4 of berries and granola.

3. Drizzle 1 tablespoon honey on each dessert and serve immediately.

PER SERVING: Calories 270; Fat Calories 25; Total Fat 3g; Saturated Fat 1.5g; Cholesterol 5mg; Sodium 115mg; Total Carbohydrates 55g; Fiber 4g; Sugars 41g; Protein 8g

## Chef's Tip:

*Raspberries are fragile. Avoid washing them under running water. Instead, wash in a bowl of water and then drain in colander.*

# Coleman BEEF

For the Coleman family, it's all about tradition. Generations of Coleman family cowboys passed down the family philosophy that delicious beef begins with a good breed of cattle carefully fed and raised – with a natural style. Coleman Angus cattle are raised without hormones or antibiotics. Fed only wholesome, residue-free grains and allowed to roam on a free range, Coleman beef is a natural product we consider Living Wise.

# Fall Menu

Panzanella

Puttanesca with Bay Scallops
and Pasta

Ciabatta

Fall Fruit Medley
with Maple Mascarpone

*Wine Recommendation*

Allegrini Valpolicella

Steele Pinot Blanc

# Puttanesca with Bay Scallops and Pasta

## Ingredients:

| | | |
|---|---|---|
| 1/2 | pound | Bay Scallops |
| 2 | tablespoons | Extra Virgin Olive Oil |
| 4 | | Anchovy Fillets, coarsely chopped |
| 2 | cloves | Fresh Garlic, minced |
| 2 | tablespoons | Capers, drained |
| 1/2 | cup | Roasted Red Peppers, cut into thin strips |
| 1/2 | cup | Kalamata Olives, pitted, coarsely chopped |
| 1 | 14.5 oz can | Tomatoes, diced in puree |
| | 8.8 oz pkg | Pappardelle Pasta, cooked al dente (ref. Chef Pasta Tip) |
| | | Black Pepper, to taste |
| | | Italian Parsley Sprigs |

## Preparation:

1. Gather all ingredients

2. Place a sauté pan on medium heat and add 1 tablespoon olive oil. When the oil begins to smoke, add scallops. Quickly flip scallops around for approximately 1 minute. Season scallops to your liking. Set aside.
   Chef's Tip: Very small pinch of Kosher salt and white pepper.

3. Place second tablespoon of olive oil in a skillet on medium heat. Add anchovies, garlic, capers, red peppers and olives. Sauté ingredients for a brief time. Add tomatoes and turn heat down to a simmer for 3 minutes. Season to your taste.

4. Just before serving, heat a large skillet on medium heat. Pour in 1 tablespoon olive oil. Add cooked and drained pasta, quickly flipping in pan to prevent burning. Season with a pinch of black pepper. Add scallops, continuing to flip pasta and scallops until hot – about 2 minutes.

5. Arrange pasta and scallops in center of platter and pour Puttanesca Sauce around the outside of the pasta and scallops. Serve immediately.

6. Garnish Tip: Italian parsley sprigs

## Chef's Tip:

*Goes famously with any type of cooked pasta; poached, baked, sautéed or grilled fresh fish or shellfish – clams, mussels, scallops or abalone.*

## Chef's Tip:
*Works well with your favorite pasta and shellfish.*

## Pasta Cooking Procedure:

1. In a sauce pot, fill ³/₄ full with water. Add a pinch of salt and a splash of olive oil. Bring to a boil.

2. Add pasta, stirring to prevent clumping and sticking. Cook approximately 7 minutes. Drain to rinse off starch. Set aside.

3. Note: When cooking pasta, the pasta will double in volume — dry stage 8 ounces, cooked stage about 16 ounces.

PER SERVING: Calories 200; Fat Calories 60; Total Fat 7g; Saturated Fat 1g; Cholesterol 45mg; Sodium 760mg; Total Carbohydrates 20g; Fiber 1g; Sugars 3g; Protein 13g

*Yield: Serves 4*

# Ciabatta

Our Ciabatta is a free-form, flat Italian bread that has a flavorful, chewy crust and soft interior.

# Panzanella

## Ingredients:

| | | |
|---|---|---|
| 4 | cups | Artisan Bread*, cut into ¹/₂ inch pieces |
| 1 | pound | Ripe Plum Tomatoes, cut into quarters |
| 1 | | Cucumber, seeds removed and cut in ¹/₂ inch pieces |
| 1 | small | Red Onion, cut into ¹/₂ inch pieces |
| 6 | large | Fresh Basil Leaves, cut in thin strips |
| ¹/₂ | cup | Pitted Kalamata Olives, chopped |
| ³/₄ | pound | Whole Milk Mozzarella, cut in ¹/₂ inch pieces |

Dressing:

| | | |
|---|---|---|
| 2 | tablespoons | Aged Balsamic Vinegar |
| 2 | tablespoons | Capers, in their liquid |
| 1 | clove | Fresh Garlic, peeled and minced |
| 1 | tablespoon | Lemon Juice |
| ¹/₂ | cup | Extra Virgin Olive Oil |

\* Rosemary-Olive Oil Artisan or
  French Baguette

## Preparation:

1. Toast Artisan Bread in 400 degree preheated oven for about 10 minutes. Remove and let cool.

2. Prepare remaining ingredients and prepare dressing as follows: Combine vinegar, capers, garlic and lemon juice in a mixing bowl. Using a wire whisk, stir ingredients briskly and slowly add oil until well blended. Refrigerate until ready to serve.

3. Just before serving, combine all ingredients.

PER SERVING: Calories 410; Fat Calories 260; Total Fat 29g; Saturated Fat 9g; Cholesterol 35mg; Sodium 880mg; Total Carbohydrates 25g; Fiber 2g; Sugars 5g; Protein 14g

*Yield:*
*Serves 4-6*

# Fall Fruit Medley
## with Maple Mascarpone

## Ingredients:

| | | | | | |
|---|---|---|---|---|---|
| 6 | | Clementines | ¹/₄ cup | | Mascarpone |
| 1 | | Banana, ripe | 2 | tablespoons | Maple Syrup |
| 1 | | Papaya, ripe | ¹/₂ cup | | Heavy Cream |
| 2 | tablespoons | Grand Marnier | ¹/₄ cup | | Chopped Pecans, toasted |

## Preparation:

1. Break 2 clementines into sections. Clean off any white rind and remove seeds.

2. Juice the other 4 clementines and put in a heavy fry pan or wok with the Grand Marnier. Bring to a boil over medium-high heat and reduce to about ¹/₄ cup of liquid (approximately 8 minutes).

3. Meanwhile, peel and slice banana. Peel, seed and cube papaya.

4. When sauce is reduced, add clementines, banana and papaya. Cook for about 3 minutes on medium heat, stirring carefully.

5. Remove from heat. Pour into a bowl and refrigerate until cool. Spoon fruit into wine glasses or other dessert glasses.

6. Prepare mascarpone by placing heavy cream, mascarpone and maple syrup in a mixing bowl. Whip until cream holds shape. Pipe or spoon on top of fruit mixture. Garnish with pecan pieces.

PER SERVING: Calories 320; Fat Calories 180; Total Fat 21g; Saturated Fat 12g; Cholesterol 70mg; Sodium 25mg; Total Carbohydrates 30g; Fiber 4g; Sugars 23g; Protein 3g

# Dry-Packed SCALLOPS

Dry-packed scallops are unlike the majority of scallops sold in the United States because they are tripolyphosphate-free. Acting as a preservative, most scallops are soaked in a solution of water and sodium tripolyphosphate to help the scallop increase its ability to hold water. Soaking helps the scallops appear shiny but can trap spoiling odors inside. By eliminating this process, dry-packed scallops maintain the deep, sweet aroma similar to fresh scallops. It's a natural product we consider Living Wise.

# Winter Menu

Sautéed Red Cabbage with Cranberries

Herb Crusted Rack of Pork

Great Northern Bean Timbale
with Green Apple Chutney

Multigrain Bread

Oven Roasted Winter Pear Crunch

*Wine Recommendation*

Jean-Luc Colombo Cotes Du Rhone

Trimbach Pinot Blanc

# Herb Crusted Rack of Pork

## Ingredients:

*Yield: Serves 4*

| | | |
|---|---|---|
| 3¹/₂-4 pounds | Rack of Pork | |
| 2 | tablespoons | |
| + 2 teaspoons | Olive Oil | |
| ¹/₂ | ounces | Fresh Thyme, chopped |
| ¹/₂ | ounces | Fresh Rosemary, chopped |
| ¹/₂ | ounces | Fresh Sage, chopped |
| 1 | tablespoon | Garlic, coarsely chopped |
| 1 | tablespoon | Sea Salt |

## Preparation:

1. When buying rack, have meat cutter French bones and leave some fat on the outside.

2. Pick herb from stems; chop coarse; place in bowl. Add chopped garlic and 2 tablespoons olive oil. Mix well.

3. Rub remaining 2 teaspoons olive oil completely over roast. Sprinkle with salt. Press or pat herb mixture over top and sides of roast (not bones).

4. Place on rack in baking dish and roast for 1.3-1.5 hours in a preheated 350 degree oven until meat thermometer reaches 155 degrees. Meat should be slightly pink in center.

5. Remove from oven and let rest for 15 minutes before carving. Carve between bones to serve.

PER SERVING: Calories 290; Fat Calories 120; Total Fat 14g; Saturated Fat 4g; Cholesterol 95mg; Sodium 250mg; Total Carbohydrates 2g; Fiber <1g; Protein 38g

## Green Apple Chutney

### Ingredients:

*Yield: 3 cups*

| | | |
|---|---|---|
| 2 | | Granny Smith Apples, peeled, seeded, coarsely chopped |
| ¹/₂ cup | | Dried Apricots, coarsely chopped |
| ¹/₃ cup | | Golden Raisins |
| 2 teaspoons | | Fresh Ginger, peeled and grated |
| ¹/₈ teaspoon | | Red Pepper Flakes |
| ¹/₂ cup | | Sugar |
| ¹/₂ cup | | Honey |
| 2 tablespoons | | Red Onion, coarsely chopped |
| 1 cup | | Apple Cider Vinegar |
| 2 teaspoons | | Sea Salt |
| ¹/₈ teaspoon | | Black Pepper |

### Preparation:

1. Combine sugar, honey and vinegar in a heavy-bottomed pot. Stir to dissolve sugar.

2. Add remaining ingredients. Reduce heat to low and simmer for 30 minutes, stirring occasionally, until chutney appears thick.

3. Serve warm.

PER SERVING: Calories 100; Total Fat 0g; Sodium 670mg; Total Carbohydrates 26g; Fiber 1g; Sugars 23g; Protein 0g

# Great Northern Bean Timbale

## Ingredients:

| | | |
|---|---|---|
| 15.5 oz can | | Great Northern Beans, rinsed and drained |
| 1 | | Whole Egg (large) |
| 1 | clove | Fresh Garlic, coarsely chopped |
| 1 | tablespoon | Fresh Parsley, coarsely chopped |
| 1 | tablespoon | Half and Half |
| Pinch | | White Pepper |

## Preparation:

1. Gather all ingredients. Preheat oven to 375 degrees. Drain beans.

2. Place all ingredients into a food processor; blend until smooth.

3. Using no-stick spray, spray the sides and bottom of timbales. Spoon bean mixture into timbales, just below the rim.

4. Pour 2 cups of water into bottom of cake pan large enough to place timbales. Place the filled timbales into the water bath. Cook on lower oven rack for approximately 35 minutes or until bean mixture springs back when gently pressed. The mixture will also pull away from the sides of the timbale.

5. Carefully pull pan from oven. Remove timbales from water bath, and with a small paring knife, carefully loosen the edges. Flip timbale over and tap sides and bottom; mixture should release.

6. Serve hot.

*Yield:*
*4 Timbales*

PER SERVING: Calories 110; Fat Calories 25; Total Fat 3g; Saturated Fat 1.5g; Cholesterol 40mg; Sodium 20mg; Total Carbohydrates 15g; Fiber 3g; Sugars <1g; Protein 6g

# Sautéed Red Cabbage with Cranberries

*Yield:*
*Serves 6-8*

## Ingredients:

| | | |
|---|---|---|
| 1 | tablespoon | Olive Oil |
| 7 | tablespoons | Brown Sugar, divided |
| 2 | tablespoons | Minced Garlic |
| 3 | cups | Fresh or Frozen Cranberries, divided |
| 1 | cup | Red Wine Vinegar |
| 2 | pounds | Red Cabbage, thinly sliced |
| | | Sea Salt, to taste |

## Preparation:

1. In large non-aluminum fry pan, heat oil and 3 tablespoons brown sugar over medium heat.

2. Add garlic; sauté 2 minutes.

3. Add 2 cups cranberries and vinegar. Cover and cook 5 minutes until cranberries pop.

4. Add cabbage. Cook and stir about 15-20 minutes until tender. Add remaining sugar; mix well and add 1 cup cranberries.

5. Remove from heat. Let stand 5 minutes until cranberries are hot and tender.

6. Salt to taste.

PER SERVING: Calories 70; Fat Calories 10; Total Fat 1g; Sodium 60mg; Total Carbohydrates 14g; Fiber 2g; Sugars 9g; Protein 1g

## Chef's Tip:

*Fresh cranberries are only available from October until December, but frozen cranberries are available year round.*

# Multigrain

Our Multigrain Bread is a mixture of healthy grains and seeds including whole wheat, rye, rolled oats, sunflower seeds and flax.

# Oven Roasted Winter Pear Crunch

## Ingredients:

*Yield:*
*4 servings*

| | | |
|---|---|---|
| 4 | | D'Anjou Pears, ripe, peeled, cored and sliced |
| ¹/₄ | cup | Dried Cranberries |
| 4 | tablespoons | Pear Liqueur or pear juice |
| 4 | tablespoons | Lemon Juice |
| ¹/₂ | teaspoon | Cinnamon |
| 1 | cup | Granola |
| ¹/₄ | cup | Honey |

## Preparation:

1. Preheat oven to 350 degrees.

2. Place pears and cranberries in a casserole and sprinkle on pear liqueur, lemon juice and cinnamon.

3. Spread granola evenly over the pears. Drizzle with honey.

4. Bake for 30-40 minutes or until pears are tender. Serve warm.

PER SERVING: Calories 220; Fat Calories 35; Total Fat 4g; Sodium 30mg; Total Carbohydrates 47g; Fiber 5g; Sugars 32g; Protein 3g

## Chef's Tip:

*Try substituting pear juice for pear liqueur.*
*Serve with vanilla ice cream.*

Look for Living Wise

signs throughout our stores

where you'll find

an extraordinary selection

of premium quality natural foods.

# We are proud

to carry the following products in our Living Wise sections.

LUND FOOD HOLDINGS, INC.